Cuando hace calor

llevo

 una camiseta

y

 unos pantalones cortos.

Cuando hace frío

llevo

 unos pantalones,

 un jersey

y  un abrigo.

Cuando llueve

llevo un paraguas.

Cuando voy a una fiesta

llevo

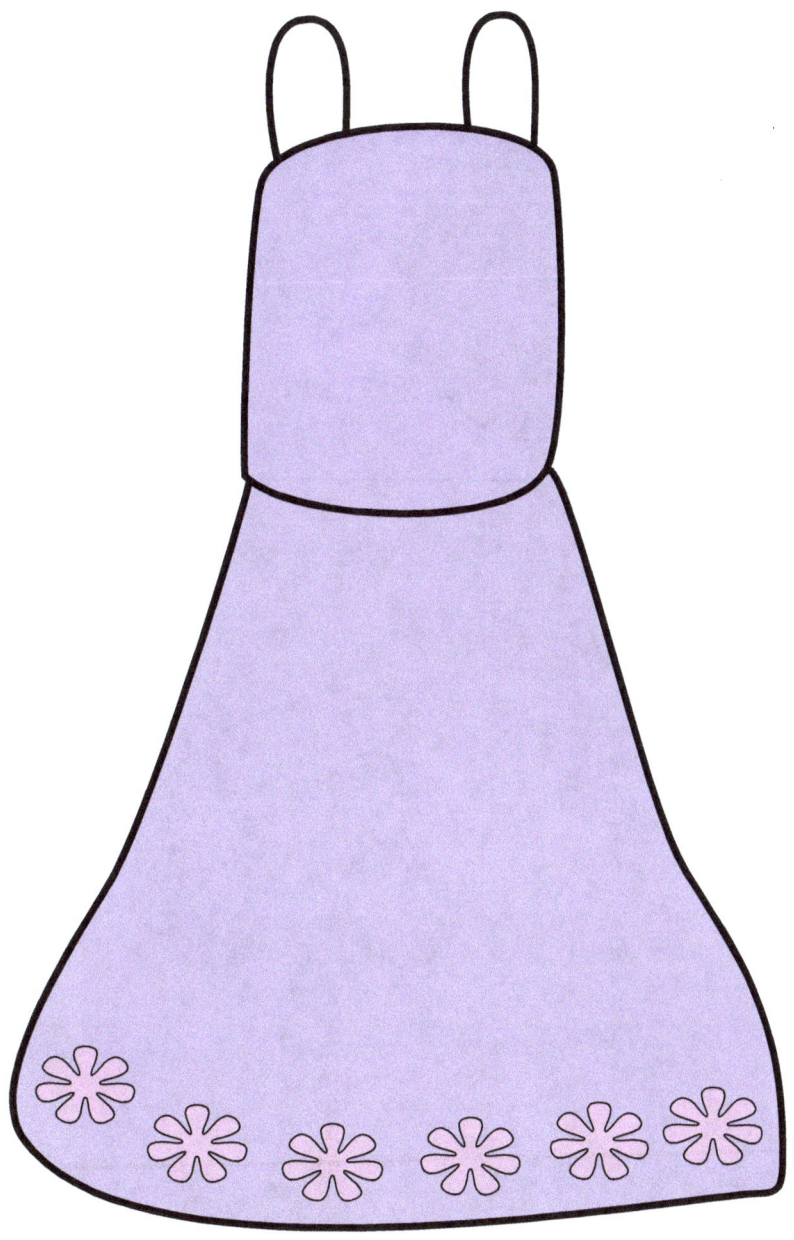

un vestido.

Cuando voy al parque

llevo

una camiseta

y

unos vaqueros.

Cuando tengo hambre

como fruta.

Cuando hay música

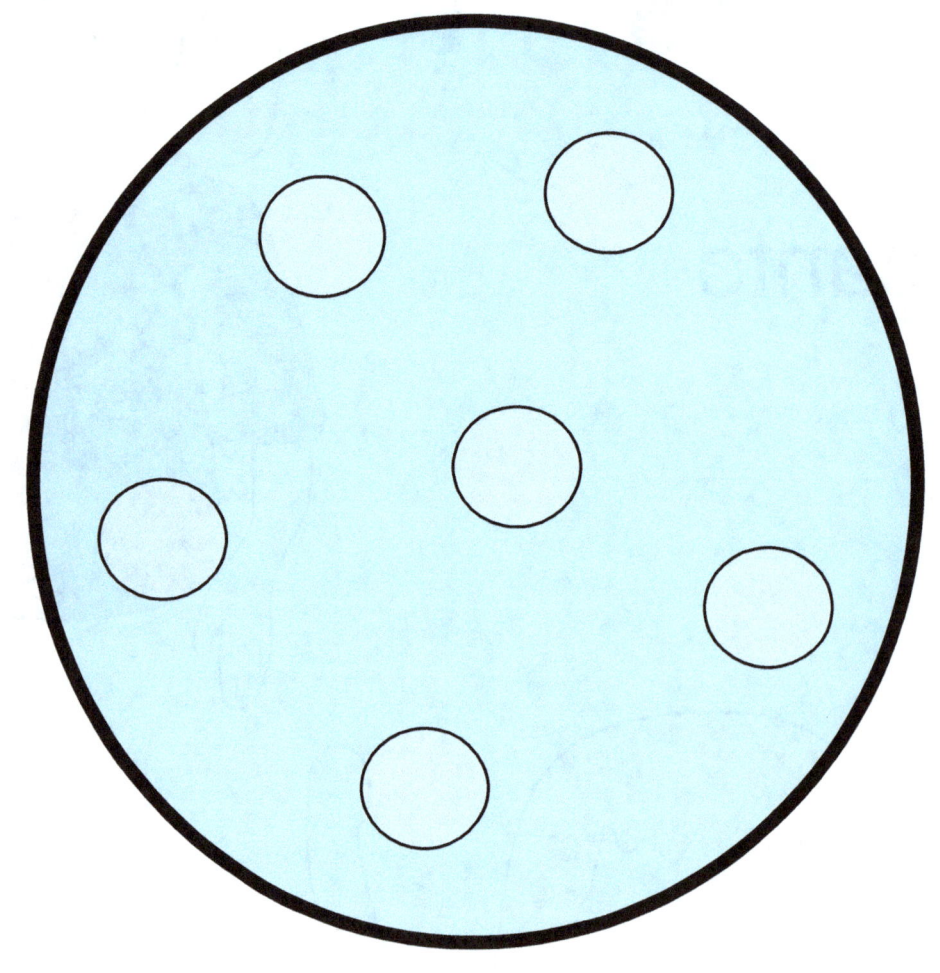

Cuando tengo un balón

juego al fútbol.

En la maleta hay…..

 fruta

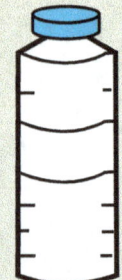 agua

 música

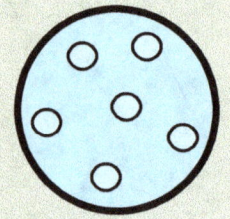 un balón

 un paraguas

 una camiseta

 un jersey

 unos vaqueros

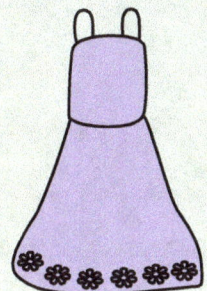 un vestido

 unos pantalones

 unos pantalones cortos

y

 un abrigo

I hope you have enjoyed this story! Try to look back at the Spanish words from time to time to help you remember them. Reviews help other readers discover my books so please consider leaving a short review on the site where the book was purchased. Your feedback is important to me. Thank you! And have fun learning Spanish! It's a lovely language to learn! Joanne Leyland

© Copyright Joanne Leyland 1st edition 2016   2nd edition 2018   3rd edition 2019   4th edition 2021
The useful Spanish words and phrases, the song lyrics and the translation of the story may be photocopied by the purchasing individual or institution for use in class or at home.   The rest of the book may not be photocopied or reproduced digitally without the prior written agreement of the author.

Useful Spanish words and phrases

a coat — un abrigo

a dress — un vestido

a jumper — un jersey

an umbrella — un paraguas

a t-shirt — una camiseta

jeans — unos vaqueros

trousers — unos pantalones

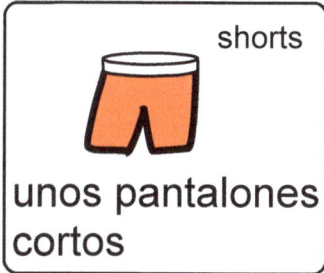
shorts — unos pantalones cortos

fruit — fruta

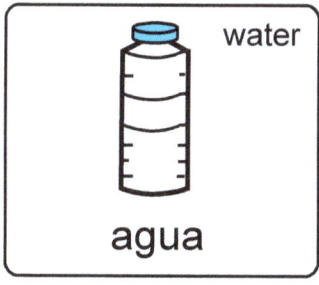
water — agua

music — música

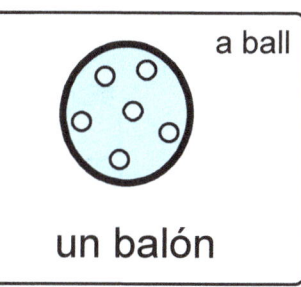
a ball — un balón

the park — el parque

a party — una fiesta

a suitcase — una maleta

a spaceship — una nave espacial

Cuando .... When

it's raining — llueve

it's cold — hace frío

it's hot — hace calor

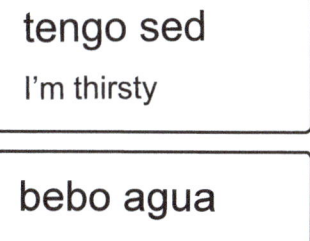
tengo sed — I'm thirsty

bebo agua — I drink water

I sing — canto

I dance — bailo

I play football — juego al fútbol

tengo hambre — I'm hungry

como fruta — I eat fruit

© Copyright Joanne Leyland - This page may be photocopied by the purchasing individual or institution for use in class or at home

Let's sing a song!

The following words could either be sung to a made up tune, or you could try saying the words as a rap.

For inspiration of a melody to use you could hum first a nursery rhyme. How many different versions can you create using the lyrics?

Cuando tengo hambre, cuando tengo hambre
Como fruta, como fruta
Cuando tengo hambre, cuando tengo hambre
Como fruta, como fruta

Cuando tengo sed, cuando tengo sed
Bebo agua, bebo agua
Cuando tengo sed, cuando tengo sed
Bebo agua, bebo agua

Cuando hace frío, cuando hace frío
Llevo un abrigo, llevo un abrigo
Cuando hace frío, cuando hace frío
Llevo un abrigo, llevo un abrigo

Cuando hace calor, cuando hace calor
Llevo una camiseta, llevo una camiseta
Cuando hace calor, cuando hace calor
Llevo una camiseta, llevo una camiseta

Cuando tengo hambre = When I'm hungry   como fruta = I eat fruit
Cuando tengo sed = When I am thirsty   bebo agua = I drink water
Cuando hace frío = When it's cold   llevo un abrigo = I wear a coat
Cuando hace calor = When it's hold   llevo una camiseta = I wear a t-shirt

The Spanish word **llevo** sounds like **yeh-boh**. (The double L is a y sound, and the v is a soft b sound)

© Copyright Joanne Leyland - This page may be photocopied by the purchasing individual or institution for use in class or at home

Spanish	English
Hola, me llamo Lucas.	Hello, my name is Luke.
Soy del planeta Marte.	I'm from the planet Mars.
Hola, me llamo Ana María.	Hello, my name is Anna Maria.
Soy de Madrid.	I'm from Madrid.
una camiseta	a t-shirt
un jersey	a jumper
unos vaqueros	some jeans
un vestido	a dress
unos pantalones	some trousers
unos pantalones cortos	some shorts
un abrigo	a coat
fruta	fruit
agua	water
música	music
un balón	a ball
un paraguas	an umbrella
¿Por qué tienes tantas cosas?	Why do you have all these things?
¡No lo entiendo!	I don't understand!
Cuando hace calor	When it's hot
llevo una camiseta y unos pantalones cortos.	I wear a t-shirt and shorts.
Cuando hace frío	When it's cold
llevo unos pantalones, un jersey y un abrigo.	I wear trousers, a jumper and a coat.
Cuando llueve	When it rains
llevo un paraguas.	I use an umbrella.
Cuando voy a una fiesta	When I go to a party
llevo un vestido.	I wear a dress.
Cuando voy al parque	When I go to the park
llevo una camiseta y unos vaqueros.	I wear a t-shirt and jeans.
Cuando tengo hambre	When I'm hungry
como fruta.	I eat some fruit.
Cuando tengo sed	When I'm thirsty
bebo agua.	I drink water.
Cuando hay música	When there's music
canto y bailo.	I sing and I dance.
Cuando tengo un balón	When I've a ball
juego al fútbol.	I play football.
Me gusta jugar al fútbol.	I like playing football.
Me gusta tu nave espacial.	I like your spaceship
Es muy grande. Es fantástica.	It's very big. It's fantastic.
Me gusta tu planeta.	I like your planet.
¿Qué hay en la maleta?	What's in the suitcase?
En la maleta hay….	In the suitcase there is…
¡Qué buena idea!	What a good idea!
Gracias. Adiós. Adiós.	Thank you. Goodbye. Goodbye.

For children learning Spanish there are also the following books by Joanne Leyland:

El Mono Que Cambia De Color

A monkey changes colour when he eats. Will he ever return to his usual colour?
Topics: General conversation, days, colours, food, opinions.

Seis Mascotas Maravillosas

Marcos doesn't have a pet. Will his wish for a pet come true?
Topics: Types of pets, colours, sizes, names of pets, opinions.

On Holiday In Spain
Cool Kids Speak Spanish

Ideal for holidays and to challenge children to speak Spanish whilst away. Topics include greetings, numbers, drinks, food, souvenirs, town, hotels & campsites.

Spanish Word Games

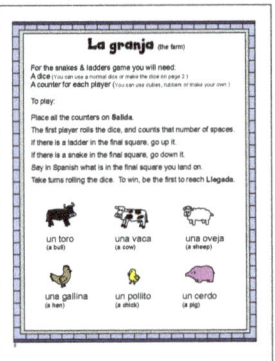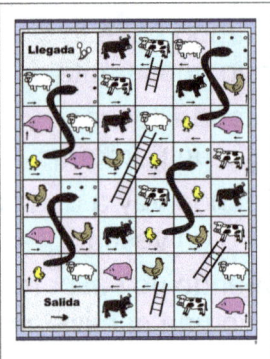

Have fun learning Spanish with this lovely collection of games. The 15 topics include fruit, the farm, ice creams, pets, hobbies, the restaurant, tapas, weather, vegetables...

Photocopiable Games For Teaching Spanish

Differentiated activities for children of various abilities. The games are colour coded according to the amount of Spanish words in each game. Games include: board games, dominoes, snakes and ladders, mini cards, 3 or 4 in a row and co-ordinates.

Topics include:
- Drinks
- Greetings
- Fruit
- Pets
- Clothes
- Food
- Transport
- Weather

For more information about learning Spanish and the great books by Joanne Leyland go to
https://funspanishforkids.com

www.ingramcontent.com/pod-product-compliance
Lightning Source LLC
Chambersburg PA
CBHW081400080526
44588CB00016B/2556